Sparky Can Fly

Sparky Can Fly. By Sandy Stream
Illustrated by Yoko Matsuoka
Edited by Tomoko Matsuoka

ISBN: 978-0-9739481-2-7

Copyright © 2014 by Sandy Stream Publishing. Montreal, Canada.
All rights reserved. No part of this book may be reproduced, stored in a retrieval system, or transmitted in any form or by any means without the written permission of Sandy Stream Publishing.

On a Personal Note

This series is illustrated not because it is for children, but rather because images are often much more powerful than words.

This series is intended to show you how similar we all are, both in our suffering and in our ability to heal. When we learn how to observe ourselves honestly and without judgment, healing and transformation occurs naturally, without any effort.

You might need, as we all do, the support of a healthy, non-judgmental friend or other helper to hold you up on your journey. I know I did. There are many healers in this world that can help guide you if you let them. Don't give up on finding one. You can feel them immediately when you meet them.

I am every character in this series. I have lived every moment of it, either directly, or by feeling what I have seen and continue to see around me. This is how we are all connected—because we can feel each other inside out.

Sandy Stream

Based on *many* true stories

Once upon a time there was a nest with three little eggs.

One summer day, a beautiful baby bird was born.

His mom called him Sparky because he had a lovely sparkle in his eyes. Sparky was a happy bird.

Sparky lived in a beautiful world. It had rainbows and sunshine and beautiful trees.

But it also had giants who did whatever they wanted. Sparky had never seen or met a giant.

Sparky couldn't wait to learn how to fly. "Mama, teach me how to fly," Sparky said.

His mama looked at him with a smile. "You do not need Mama to teach you how to fly. You already know how. Just listen to your wings. They will show you the way."

One terrible and dark evening, while Mama and Sparky were cuddling in their nest, a big giant came and grabbed Sparky.

The giant brought him to his castle and put him in a cage.

Tweet! Tweet! "Somebody help me!"
Tweet! Tweet!

But no one could hear the little bird. Sparky was very scared. He spent the night alone.

The next day Sparky tried again.

Tweet! Tweet!

Suddenly Sparky heard someone coming! It was the giant! Sparky was really scared. He stopped tweeting. He held it in his throat and was very, very still.

The giant came closer to Sparky.
He gave Sparky yummy food.
Sparky wasn't sure what to do, but he was really hungry.

The next day, the giant came to see Sparky again. He brought more yummy food.

Sparky sat on his finger. The giant asked Sparky to sing.
Sparky slowly started to sing his favorite song.

But the giant didn't like Sparky's song at all! He put Sparky back in his cage and slammed the door.

Sparky was afraid. He didn't know what to do…

Boom! Boom! Boom! Boom!

His heart was beating so fast. He wanted to tweet for help!

Boom! Boom! Boom! Boom!

But he knew no one would hear him, so he held it in. The tweet in his throat got bigger.

I have to get away!! Sparky told himself. He felt a huge wave of energy run throughout his body, as if he had a little tornado inside of him—ready to do anything!

But he couldn't escape, or fight…
He couldn't do anything.
He was frozen in place.
The tornado in Sparky stayed locked inside.

Many days passed.
And so it was that on some days the giant was happy and kind and would give Sparky yummy food.

On other days he caressed Sparky.

On other days the giant **ROARED** when Sparky didn't do things the way the giant wanted.

Sparky always froze when the giant was angry. He couldn't do anything.

Every day, Sparky tried to be nice so the giant wouldn't get too mad.
But even when Sparky was on his best behavior, the giant would sometimes get very angry.

Sparky was confused.
He didn't know if tomorrow the giant would take him out, be nice, or be mad.

One day, the giant decided to take Sparky to the fair. Sparky loved the fair!
Whenever the giant took Sparky out, he held Sparky in his hands.

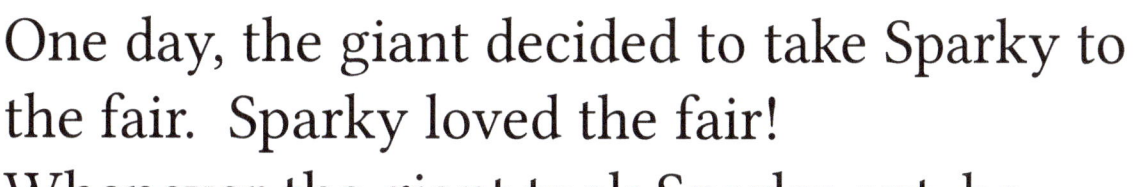

The giant always held Sparky's wings when they went out because Sparky was not allowed to fly.

Many seasons passed.
Sparky grew bigger and bigger.
Slowly, he became somewhat used to being with the giant.

But at night, he wondered about other birds.
He knew that other birds could fly.
Could he fly too? He couldn't remember whether he had ever learned to fly.

Then one day, like any other day, Sparky was playing in his cage when he realized his beak was longer. He could reach the lock and open his cage! What should he do?

He was too scared of getting caught, so he quickly closed the door and locked the cage.

The next day, when the giant was out, Sparky opened the cage again. He went to the edge and tried to fly.

He fell...

and fell...

and fell...

... all the way to the ground.
He didn't know how to fly!
It took many tries for Sparky to get back in his cage. When he finally got back in, he was trembling.

Pheuff! The giant didn't see him. He would have been very, very mad if he had seen Sparky outside the cage!
Sparky didn't open the door again for a long, long time.

When spring arrived, the giant left the window near the cage open. Sparky could see a lovely yellow bird land on a branch near the window.

Sparky wished he could see the sun and feel the wind as the yellow bird could!

So he gathered his courage and strength and fell out of the cage. Then he flew with all his might to the edge of the window. He smelled the fresh air...

But he could not fly out.
He was too scared, too confused.
If he left, would he miss the giant?
How far could he fly?
What if the giant found him after he flew away? He was frozen again.

Sparky did not notice the giant coming. The giant snatched him and squeezed him really hard.

He threw Sparky back in the cage and told him never to try that again OR ELSE! Sparky didn't open the cage again for a long time...

...until one day, when Sparky thought he heard his mother's voice from the window.

Mama?

What should Sparky do?
He was frozen again...
Sparky looked down at his feathers.
They weren't moving.

Then he remembered what Mama had said about flying. *Just listen to your wings. They will show you the way.* His wings fluttered just a bit. He was so scared.

Boom! Boom! Boom! Boom!

His wings fluttered just a bit again.
His wings were giving him the answer.
He knew what to do...!

He took a deep breath and opened the lock...
He felt his muscles strengthen and the tornado inside him rise.
He let his fury expand and felt its power.
Then Sparky finally unleashed it all—and did what he had wanted to do for so long...

WOOOSH!

He flew out of the cage,
flew out of the window,
and into his new life…
never looking back.

The beginning

The River Series

Sparky Can Fly
Sparky's Mama
Tweets and Hurricanes
Feathers
Flex
Roots
The River

www.RiverSpeaks.com

www.ingramcontent.com/pod-product-compliance
Lightning Source LLC
Chambersburg PA
CBHW060520300426
44112CB00017B/2741